Good Life Habits

A Short Guide To 10 Simple Life Habits For Everyday Fulfillment

Introduction

Let me start off by a greeting, a show of gratitude, and an applause. My name is Richard K. Takayama and I want to thank you and congratulate you for picking up my book, "Good Life Habits: A Short Guide To 10 Simple Life Habits For Everyday Fulfillment."

Do you ever feel stuck? Do you feel like no matter where you are in life, you lack that sense of self-actualization and fulfillment? Like you wake up and you have nothing to motivate you to get out of bed? I have been there also, and I hope what I have to offer in the following pages can help you out.

Many people associate happiness and fulfillment with "flashy" things like riches and fame. True, these aspects are very eye-catching and looks like something that would feel nice to have, but it's important to recognize what they really are. There are merely a couple of aspects. Two amongst so much more.

Looking back at my life, I feel that building *fulfillment* is like building your own *Parthenon*. The beautiful temple in Greece had 69 stone columns to support itself. How many columns you need to build your temple of *fulfillment* is up to you, but here is my first piece of advice. Build *multiple* columns and build them *strong*. Life tends to push you around. Sometimes the "push" becomes too strong and a few of your columns may collapse. Having the support of the remaining columns will help you in those rough times. Having just a few "flashy" columns, like money and fame, are not enough for you to stand strong when the going gets tough (and the they tend to be rather fragile too).

So, let's start by building ten. This book will focus on 10 simple habits that will help you build your temple of fulfillment. By building the columns brick by brick through your daily activities, they will become sturdier and more reliable.

Again, thank you for choosing this book. I hope you enjoy it!

Table of Contents

Part 1: The Mind

"A healthy mind observes and questions itself. This is the path to inner peace and happiness. Don't believe everything you think."
~Vironika Tugaleva

Let's start with habits that focus on improving your *mind* because this is where everything begins.

Chapter 1: Practicing Meditation

Meditation entails being in 'thoughtless awareness'. It is a state of being aware- you are either in this state or not. In other words, meditation is a mental exercise that works to regulate attention either to internal or external factors or to whatever is predominant in the present moment.

You might feel like you lack direction, or your life is just super stressful, or you simply cannot seem to focus on any task that comes by. Meditation can help you do this and much more.

Why Meditate…

Some of the benefits of meditation include:

To manage stress

Stress keeps you on edge and makes you all negative and grumpy (if not depressed). Negativity is a major enemy of feeling fulfilled, as you tend to focus on all the wrong things. This means that you cannot effectively move forward in life. More specifically, stress can lead to depression, anxiety, high blood pressure. Simply, you just feel horrible when you are stressed.

A study by the General Hospital Psychiatry shows that meditation significantly reduces stress if you consistently practice it for 3 months. This was because the subjects of the study became calmer and were able to critically think about their stress triggers; hence, come up with sensible solutions.

Another study shows a type of meditation known as mindful meditation that helps you alleviate stress related inflammations especially of the brain. Mindfulness creates an environment for the mind that is 100% incompatible with anxiety. Mindfulness also lowers this inflammation through alteration of the expression of pro-inflammatory genes (genes involved in inflammation).

Enhancing Self-Awareness

Some forms of meditation, e.g. self-inquiry meditation, is majorly focused on helping you understand yourself thus helping you grow into the best version of yourself. Some other forms show you how to recognize those habits that are either self-defeating or harmful.

A Study on such meditation was conducted on 21 women fighting breast cancer who were subjected to a tai chi program. This program boosted their self-esteem more than the women who were receiving social support sessions. This was because tai chi involves a range of movements and meditation that helps you be in touch with your actual self. The reason as to this is because tai chi enables better neural integration which results in behaviors that are more resilient as well as a deep level of interpersonal and intra personal harmonization.

Hence, the women were able to easily accept that they had breast cancer and not feel sorry for themselves; this boosted their self-esteem.

Makes you kinder

Other types of meditation such as Metta/loving kindness meditation particularly teach you how to generate/ increase positive feelings towards others and yourself. It is a gradual process that helps you start extending kindness and forgiveness to friends, acquaintances and then finally to enemies.

As I'll explain later in the book, healthy relationships are a major factor when it comes to living a fulfilled life and meditation is one way to help you nurture those relationships.

Twenty-two studies conducted on this form of meditation have proved that it increases people's ability to be compassionate towards others and themselves. These kinds of meditation adopt the use of mantras relating to kindness (and positive thoughts) which when said over and over become part of your reality.

Studies showed that the more effort you put into Metta meditation the more effective it becomes.

Having understood the benefits of meditation, let us now learn how you should meditate.

How to Meditate for Everyday Fulfillment

First things first, prepare! This includes yourself and the place you will be meditating in.

Prepare your mind for a session by knowing your purpose for meditating; whether it's to reduce stress, find inner peace or simply achieve calmness, have that reason at the back of your mind.

Prepare your environment by choosing a calm and quiet space and enhance your set-up by adding soothing ornaments such as a scented candle. Also, ensure that the time you choose is convenient and free from distractions (like trying to meditate when your kids are screaming for food is probably not a good idea).

Make meditation a lifestyle by practicing it daily but not pressuring yourself to practice it daily. Essentially, you should try to take even if it's just ten minutes in the morning (or some other convenient time) to meditate. If you are unable to or you aren't just feeling it you can skip a day but try to make it consistent.

Meditation Techniques for a Healthy Mind and Life

These can be generally categorized into:

Focused Attention Meditation

This involves focusing on something in particular for a whole meditation session. It can be a mantra, a part of your body, a feeling; it all depends on what you are trying to achieve here.

For instance, if you want to develop a certain feeling then you focus on that feeling. Examples of such type of meditation include chakra meditation, mantra meditation, loving kindness and Buddhist meditation.

For focused attention meditation, follow these steps

1. Stretch to get rid of any tension and sit with your legs crossed (place your hands wherever you are most comfortable).

2. Tilt your head as if you are facing downwards to help ease your breathing by opening up your chest.

3. Set your timer depending on the length of your session. Breathe in and out, slowly.

4. Now go ahead and solely focus on that particular thing that you want to. As I said earlier, it could be a certain feeling, a mantra, a body part, etc. it all depends on what you want to achieve.

5. Once time is up, don't just stop immediately. Bring your mind back slowly and take at least 2 minutes to enjoy the peace!

NB: If your mind happens to wander, acknowledge it and immediately take your mind back to the meditation zone.

Open Monitoring

This category involves those types of meditation that monitor all aspects of your session without any judgment or attachment. In other words, both external (e.g. sound) and internal (e.g. feelings) perceptions are seen for exactly what they are. Techniques in this category are such as Mindfulness and Vipassana meditation.

For open monitoring meditation, follow these steps:

1. Follow steps 1 to 3 of focused attention meditation then bring your mind to the now and focus on your breathing.

2. Intently focus on how the air moves in and out of your nose or how your lungs expand and contract making sure that you don't attach any judgment to the process.

3. Now move to the #5 step of focused attention meditation.

Effortless Presence (Pure Being)

This is meditation where your attention depends on itself i.e. it is not focused on anything in particular; this is actually the point of all types of meditation. They all train you to reach this level where you effortlessly dive into deep states of inner peace and consciousness.

The steps for this meditation are similar to the rest but when it comes to actually doing it, you don't control your breath, you don't try to control or force your thoughts and you don't dwell on the fact that you are meditating, you simply are.

Chapter 2: Adopting Simple Living

Believe it or not, a simple life equals a happy life. Whoever said that '*too much of everything is poisonous*' was totally right. No, just think about it, too many options/choices make us unhappy, too much food makes us unhealthy hence unhappy, too many activities distract and stress us averting any real fulfillment etc. the list is just endless. You should therefore aim to simplify your life.

Some of the ways to do this include:

De-cluttering

This simply means that you get rid of the excess stuff that has little to no use or value at all. We all have furniture, utensils, books, clothes etc. that we no longer use but still keep. De-cluttering is necessary to keep you happy and fulfilled because for starters, it is annoying to look at clutter (you've probably had your basement overflow with stuff at one point).

Secondly, it can dredge up a number of not so good emotions. For instance, stress due to lack of organization, or guilt because you don't wear half of the clothes you own or emotional baggage due to something from an ex that you hold on to.

Third, clutter has an intense impact on our brains; more specifically, it dampens performance and induces stress. According to a study conducted at Princeton University by Neuroscientists, the reason for this is that physical clutter around us competes for our attention, which negatively affects information processing and productivity.

The Bottom line is, the negative surpass the positive when it comes to clutter.

De-cluttering guidelines

- If you haven't worn something for over a year or you are keeping some clothes to wear someday e.g. when you lose weight then it's got to go.

- If something triggers bad memories or makes you feel bad then let it go.

- If there is a piece of furniture or kitchen item that doesn't serve a functional purpose then, you guessed it right, it has to go!

- If you have sentimental items that weigh down on you, as hard as it might be, you have to let them go if you want to be happy.

I guess you now get the drift.

Clear out your calendar

Logically, as humans, we dread missing opportunities. Currently, you might have your calendar booked every day; meetings, events, lunches, trips and so on. However, you need to take a breather.

There is nothing wrong with planning but, you also need to reboot. Think about how you feel after hours (or days) of working with little to no rest. Well, having everyday occupied with something to do is basically programming your mind that there is no time to rest.

It will not hurt you to skip a few pages off your calendar. During these glory days, do something that you really love or just relax (a movie and some popcorns perhaps?).

DIY- Do It Yourself

In the book shaping the dream by Israelmore Ayivor,

"You don't expect the goat to hatch the hen's eggs. People do what they know very well. Don't expect someone who doesn't know what you know to do it for you. Do it yourself."

In this consumer driven world, knowing how to do things yourself can simplify your life drastically. Not only that, but there is nothing more fulfilling than learning how to depend on yourself. For instance:

- Learn how to garden and grow your own food- saves you trips to the grocery store and long lines and all sorts of inconveniences (you will also eat healthy effortlessly).

- Learn how to knit and sew- you can make yourself or your kid a pretty scarf or you can use knitting to unwind and clear your mind.

- Learn how to fix things around the house e.g. plumbing, leaky taps, furniture etc.

- Do your own hair and basic grooming such as nails; it will save you a few bucks.

Simply put, learn how to depend on yourself more and you will love how empowered and happy you will feel.

It all comes down to you

When it comes your life and fulfillment, you should also develop a mentality that it all depends on you i.e. you are solely responsible for your happiness and fulfillment.

Instead of blaming other people and other things, make it your responsibility to be happy and fulfilled (and since you are reading this, it is safe to say that you are on the right path).

This is literally the simplest route you can take towards fulfillment.

Chapter 3: Minimizing Screen Time

By minimizing on screen time I simply mean less of TV, your phone, laptop, tablet, desktop and anything else that gives you access to virtual entertainment- well unless you are a software developer or work at Google.

According to the book, The Power of Full Engagement:

"Television, for example, is one of the primary means by which most people relax and recover. For the most part, however, watching television is the mental and emotional equivalent of eating junk food. It may provide a temporary form of recovery, but it is rarely nutritious and it is easy to consume too much. Researchers such as Mihaly Csikszentmihalyi have found that prolonged television watching is actually correlated with increased anxiety and low-level depression."

The book lists reducing screen time as a core contributor to high achievement.

In addition, too much screen time negatively affects your health. It leads to obesity (as you stay seated for most part of your day and munch on junk food) and shortens your life. It also creates anxiety as it makes you want to keep on buying (due to those exiting ads) and makes you chase artificial beauty and fame as key elements towards your happiness.

Let us now look at how you can actually minimize screen time

How to Minimize Screen Time

Start by cutting your screen time by half. If you spend around 9 hours on screens a day, cut it to 4 and a half. It might be hard at a first but once you get the hang of it, it comes easy (if necessary, don't pay for cable at first).

According to Brian Tracy:

"When you leave your television off for extended periods of time, you break the habit of watching television — and you will hardly miss it at all. Your television can be an excellent servant, but it's a terrible master. The choice is yours."

Read a book instead

Reading a book, even if it is fiction, is much better than watching a movie. First off, it's easy on your eyes and secondly it broadens your mind to be more creative as all scenarios are left to your imagination. Get yourself some physical good reads or even read on Kindle, Amazon etc.

Use a 'stupid' phone

If you always have your face glued to your phone, maybe watching cat videos, checking your social media accounts etc. then you know that a smart phone can occupy a significant amount of your time. It is easy to get distracted on ongoing trends, and all this wastes your time and sometimes it makes you feel not so good.

Old phones, which don't have the luxury of being endowed with such features, could really help.

De-clutter your devices

If you must use your smart phone (for maybe checking your mail) then you might want to delete some apps especially social media such as Facebook, Instagram, Twitter, Quora etc. (don't worry you were just fine when you didn't have them).

You might also want to close those 20 tabs that you keep open on your phone or laptop that you have been swearing that you are going to read for 4 months. Just like physical clutter, virtual clutter fights for our attention and ends up inducing feelings of guilt and stress.

I usually had at least 15 tabs open on my phone and whenever I opened my browser, I always felt guilty because I knew I saved those tabs for a good reason- but I never read them. Deleting the tabs gave me a sigh of relief (I actually didn't remember what most of the tabs were about).

Get a hobby

This is a sure way to ensure you get out of the house- well unless your hobby is writing and reading. Assess yourself (meditation can help here) and find out what you really love doing. Go for that hobby that excites you and you would not want to miss an opportunity to engage in it.

Maybe its painting, playing the piano, playing football, hiking, writing etc. make sure it's something you love. Not only will it minimize on screen time, but it will also make you happy, and who knows, you could end up building a solid career off your hobby.

Hangout with your loved ones

Another amazing way to spend your free time is spending it with friends and/or family. As you know *'laughter is good for the soul'* and there is no way you can hang out with a bunch of people that mean a lot to you and not have a good laugh.

The next time you feel like you have nothing to do other than watch a movie, call a friend and relative or friend to hang out. Trust me, you will feel much better than you would have sitting alone watching a movie.

The bottom line is, less screen time enables you to live in the moment, which enables you to enjoy each part of your life. If this is not the definition of a good life, then I don't know what is!

Chapter 4: Having a Morning Routine

'You will never change your life until you change something you do daily. The secret of your success is found in your daily routine.'~ John C. Maxwell

Have you ever had one of those days where you wake up late, spill your coffee or have a fight with your partner just before going to work? How did the rest of your day go? Having a bad morning leads to a bad day.

In fact, a study published in the journal *Academy of Management* showed that our morning moods are capable of determining how we see the rest of the day's events. The law of attraction has a little influence in this in that, when you are feeling negative, you align yourself with negative energies meaning this is simply what you will be experiencing.

Of course, moods can change and actually they do change, but it is way easier staying in a good mood than trying to set right a bad one, and the best way to do this is to ensure that you are in a good mood from the word go- right from when you get out of bed.

Guidelines For an Effective Morning Routine

Before we move on to how you can come up with a morning ritual, there are 3 guidelines you need to consider:

Start smart- According to the author of *the Power of Habit,* Charles Duhigg, the best time to start new habits (in this case a morning ritual) is during vacation. On a normal setting, you are inclined to follow that routine. However, in a dissimilar setting, you are more open to taking up new patterns of behavior. Therefore, for the morning routine, you can start it on a weekend or during vacation to practice before it gets real.

Be realistic- Don't overload yourself, make a ritual that is feasible in your current situation and lifestyle. A 5-minute ritual can proof to be as effective as a 1-hour ritual- it all depends on the above.

Have consistency- That's what the word 'ritual' is all about. Committing to your daily morning routine can help you stay on the bandwagon long enough to make it part of your life style.

How to Develop a Powerful and Effective Morning Routine

Wake up around 2 hours before you have to go anywhere

I don't mean that you necessarily have to wake up super early. Just try to wake up 2 hours before you have to be anywhere - work, school meeting etc. This will give you ample time to focus on yourself and feed your mind, spirit and body before your day commences. You can take this time to meditate or have a healthy breakfast or just anything to nurture yourself.

This point is especially important because it is nearly impractical to form a morning routine when you are in a hurry.

Practice everyday gratitude

There is no better way to start your day than being grateful. Practicing gratitude automatically makes you a happier person because you get to appreciate your life and be positive about it.

You can say aloud what you are grateful for when you wake up or you can write down everything that you are grateful for- either way works magic. Journaling can be helpful here.

Read something inspiring

Instead of watching the news or going through your email with the risk of getting negative news, read something inspiring in the morning to keep you uplifted. Take half an hour or start with 10 to 15 minutes to read or even listen to an audio book of something uplifting.

This is to help fuel your motivation and self-confidence; the positivity you will feel will do this and so much more.

One other amazing morning ritual you can adopt is choosing to work out in the morning- to boost those endorphins.

Part 2: The Body

"Take care of your body. It's the only place you have to live." ~ Jim Rohn

Chapter 5: Eating Healthy

Eating healthy is one of those things that everyone knows is a good daily habit but only a few of us practice it. Why is that? This is because most of us do not see our diet as an important part of our daily habits.

Eating healthy should be part of your lifestyle if you want to be happy. I mean, food is the fuel for your body so why would you want to use the worst kind of fuel to run it if you can't for your car?

A healthy diet gives us more energy and increases our productivity. More so, it makes us feel good about ourselves because it means that we are taking care of ourselves (I really doubt that you feel good after eating junk the whole day).

If you live by the excuse that you don't know how to eat healthy, just stop it. We all know what real food is: veggies, nuts, meat, fish, eggs etc. Once you understand how much influence your diet has on your life; energy, mood and happiness then you will instantly start being mindful of what you eat.

How Our Diet Affects Our Lives

The food that we eat gives our bodies fuel to function properly. In this context, when we eat unhealthy foods (e.g. junk food) our body is unable to function effectively. Some of the areas affected by this include:

Your Weight- When it comes to managing your weight, your diet plays the most important role (it is said diet plays 80% while exercise plays 20%).

Eating unhealthy food or too much food can lead to being overweight as you end up eating more calories than you actually burn (unhealthy foods are usually high in calories e.g. a Big Mac has 540 calories). You also eat more frequently because most unhealthy foods such as chips, French fries, donuts, cake etc are not as filling.

Your Energy Levels – Most unhealthy foods are high in sugar; hence, when you eat such foods, you experience quick spikes of energy followed by a rapid drop because sugar energy is depleted quickly.

The Aging Process - First off sugar is your skin's enemy. Once sugar gets into your bloodstream, it attaches to the proteins found there through a process known as glycation. The result of this is damaged AGE (advanced glycation end) which leads to dull skin due to damaged collagen and elastin.

The point I am trying to drive home is that an unhealthy diet leads to tons of complications to your health which can prevent you from living the life you want.

How to Eat Healthy

Without following a planned out diet, eating healthy entails:

Eat lots of veggies and fruits

The recommended amount of fruit and vegetables is 5 portions (consisting of a variety). You can chop up a banana for breakfast, have some baby carrots at lunch, have a glass or 2 of 100% fruit juice etc.

Include more fish

Fish serve as a great source of protein and is endowed with tons of minerals and vitamins such as vitamin A, B and D, potassium and iodine. Oily fish also contains omega 3 fats, which can help to prevent heart disease. They are also great for improved functioning of the brain.

Some of the fish you could try out are sardines, salmon, trout, tuna, cod etc.

Reduce intake of unhealthy fat and sugar

Our bodies do need fats but the healthy type such as olive oil, coconut oil, avocados, oily fish etc. Eating the wrong kind of fat like vegetable oil, margarine etc, will only serve to increase the bad cholesterol levels and this can lead to heart disease.

You should also limit your intake of sugar owing to the spikes in energy it causes. Reduce your intake of pastries, ice creams, fizzy drinks etc and opt to meet your sweet tooth desires from fruits.

Drink more water

Every chance you get, go ahead and gobble down some water. Water equals life. You could also eat water-based fruits such as watermelons to increase your water intake. You can also cut up pieces of fruits and vegetables like watermelon, lemon, cucumber etc and place them in the water if you do not like plain water.

Chapter 6: Working Out

As Dr. Bob Butler said,

'If there was a drug that provided all the benefits that exercise does, the whole world would be taking it.'

Exercise has many benefits for both our physical health and emotional health. Of course, you know that exercising keeps you healthy but do you also know that it makes you happy.

When you engage in physical activity, a hormone known as dopamine (a chemical that plays a role in happiness) is released as a neurotransmitter to the brain. Exercising also boosts your confidence dramatically. When you exercise and look at how good you look, your self-esteem bursts through the roof. Not only that, but exercising also makes you stronger- as you burn fat and build muscles.

When it comes to working out ensure that you:

Start slowly

If you have not been exercising regularly and you want to start doing so then start small (don't go to the gym for 2 hours and lift weights). Start with say 7 minute routines then work your way upwards until you adopt it in your daily routine; it will be easier if you exercise at the same time daily to make it a habit and build a routine.

Warm up before exercising

Take 5 to 10 minutes before working out to warm up- target those muscles you plan to exercise. For instance, you can walk for 5 minutes before a lower body workout or going for a run.

Include strength/resistance training

You should engage in resistance training for at least 2 days in a week to strengthen those muscles. Strength training usually involves resistance bands, free weights, or your own body weight (with exercises such as planks, squats and push-ups) - so you can also do it at home.

Start by doing upper and lower body workouts a day for each then work to increase those days as you get used to exercising.

Mix up your exercises

Varying your exercises keeps things interesting and can help you stay on track. In addition to that, it will ensure that you are engaging your whole body.

A good example of such a switch up is jogging on Monday, swim laps on Tuesday, riding your bike on Wednesday and so on. Don't target the same muscle group 2 days in a row. Muscles need time to recover and overworking them can cause injury.

Don't just stop

After a workout, don't just stop immediately. You need to ease your body from the workout state to the resting state. Take a 5 to 10 minutes' walk or simply stretch out your muscles before you completely rest. This can help you recover and improve your flexibility.

Generally, make it fun

Also make sure you make the whole thing fun for you. There is no point in running if you utterly hate it- you will just end up quitting in the end. If you like swimming then swim, if you like running or hiking or aerobics then do it!

Chapter 7: Having Adequate Sleep

When we think of daily habits, sleep rarely makes the list. But developing a sleep routine is really essential. According to a study published by Harvard Medical School, among other factors, sleep is important for:

Your mood - Inadequate sleep can result in impatience, moodiness, irritability, greater negative emotional reactivity and the inability to concentrate. This may be due to increased amygdala activity (a part of the brain relating to experiences of negative emotions like rage and anger) and a disconnection between the amygdale and its regulator.

Your memory and learning capability - Sleep enhances your memory through the brain's hippocampus and neocortex (that part of the brain that stores long-term memories). When you sleep, the hippocampus replays the events of your day for the neocortex which reviews and processes memories enabling them to last for the long term.

Your digestive system - Sleep has an effect on the hormones ghrelin (appetite stimulant) and leptin (appetite suppressant). Without sleep, your brain reduces production of leptin and raises ghrelin- well this can be an explanation for midnight snacking.

How to Get More Sleep

Now that you know sleep is important, how do you ensure you get adequate sleep?

Have a sleep schedule

Our bodies crave consistency. Try to sleep and wake up at the same time every day to help your body's internal clock to optimize your sleeping time. Chose that time you normally feel tired to sleep so that you don't toss and turn forcing yourself to sleep

Getting enough sleep means that you will be able to wake up without an alarm- if not, you need an earlier bed time.

Control light exposure

Melatonin is a naturally resulting hormone controlled by exposure to light to help us regulate our sleep-wake cycle. When it is dark, your brain amps up on secretion of melatonin (which makes you sleepy) and secretes less when there is light (making you more alert).

Therefore, at night keep your room dark, avoid using bright screens at night and say no to watching TV late at night (back with the TV thing again).

Watch what you eat

Your eating habits in the hours before you sleep play a role on your quality of sleep. If you are the type to indulge in caffeine during the day to keep you awake then avoid doing this around 6 to 8 hours before bedtime- as you might end up staying awake longer without falling asleep

Also, avoid big meals 3 hours before you sleep. You might experience discomfort and in the case of acidic or spicy foods, heartburn and stomach problems, which might keep you up. A lot of water at night could also mean countless bathroom trips at night, which can interfere with your sleep schedule.

Exercise

The benefits of exercising run deep. A work out can improve your sleep in a number of ways including muscle tension relief. However, don't work out just before bedtime as exercise can make you more energized- as stated earlier.

Relax

Have a hot bath, drink some warm milk, meditate as you lay in bed, finish any next day preparations an hour before you sleep, anything to ensure that you are relaxed and ready for bed.

Let us look at another habit:

Part 3: Your Social Life

"You can influence, direct and control your own environment. You can make your life what you want it to be." ~Napoleon Hill

Chapter 8: Having Healthy Relationships

As Robert Waldinger reported on the longest study on happiness ever conducted (The Grant Study), good relationships keep us happy and healthy. The study simply followed the lives of 724 people and the results remained constant.

Good relationships can keep us happy and healthy due to a number of reasons such as healthier behaviors, having a greater sense of purpose, love and support, better stress management etc.

The number of relationships you have does not matter, the quality of your relationships is what is important. How do you feel after having a good evening with the boys or girls? How do you feel after a good vacation with your family? Social connections are really important so we have to find ways to ensure that we maintain healthy ones.

First, you might be having negative relationships in your life, which just bring you down and make you unhappy. Take the following steps to deal with such negative relationships:

Try to fix the relationship

Things change, people change, its life. However, it doesn't necessarily mean that you change the people in your life because of this. When you decide to take this action, communication is your biggest asset.

Find an appropriate time and place and have a heart to heart conversation with the person you want to fix things with. If they care about you, trust me they will listen. Clearly explain that you do not want to change them in any way, you simply want to change how things are between you because currently you are not so happy. Listen to them too.

Take a break from the relationship

Sometimes we just need to clear our heads. It can be a bit hard to regard something without being biased when you are in it. If you are between the fence about ending or mending a relationship, or if you have tried fixing it with no avail then this can help.

Communication is still essential if you hope to mend things; don't just disappear on the person. Tell them why you need a break and again, if they care about you they will understand.

During your break, try to think clearly about that relationship. If it does more damage than good or if you have relentlessly tried to make things better and things don't seem to change either way then you might want to let go of such a relationship. If there is a chance then move to the fixing step.

Cutting ties

You owe it to yourself to have happy connections with people. If you feel like you have utterly done your best and still it is not working then it is time to cut them loose.

Sometimes the end of something (a relationship here) can mean a new stronger and supportive relationship.

How to Maintain Good Existing Relationships

In any relationship, whether it is a partner, a child, a parent, a friend, a work mate (or playmates as Robert Waldinger called them) maintaining healthy communication is important. This can entail:

- Reaching out to them if you have not talked in a while

- Spending more time with them

- Clearly speaking out your issues

- Date nights etc.

Also, remember to do and act just as you would like the other person to do and act.

Chapter 9: Lending A Helping Hand

"The unselfish effort to bring cheer to others will be the beginning of a happier life for ourselves." ~Helen Keller

Giving and volunteering has immense benefits on the community and people in need but it can also have greater benefits to you. If you are doing it with a genuine heart (and not due to social pressures) volunteering can make you more fulfilled, happier and healthier.

Studies have shown that this can be due to the promotion of social interactions, physical activity and good feelings (due to release of dopamine) that come from making a positive impact on someone. Some of the ways volunteering and giving makes your life better include:

Connection to others

Taking time to volunteer enables you to expand your network, meet new friends and enhance your social skills. When you commit to a shared activity with other people, you are able to closely associate with people hence making new friends and even strengthening already existing ones.

If you also find it hard to meet new people, volunteering helps you do this without really doing anything. You simply have to show up and you will end up meeting people you have similar interests with (volunteering is one of them!).

Mind and body well being

The aspect of social contact while working and helping others can have a profound benefit on your mood and even relieve stress. A meaningful connection with someone is the cause for this. As explained earlier, being helpful brings immense pleasure to people (due to increased levels of dopamine).

Also, as you get to work with others who are less fortunate, you get to be more grateful for who you are and what you have. An attitude of gratitude is all it takes to lead a positive life.

You are also more physically active when you volunteer. You certainly walk and move more than you would have if you just 'chilled'.

You have fun!

Volunteering can be a way to explore your passions and interests. When you volunteer in something you find important, it can be a sort of escape from day to day routine and personal commitments. It also provides you with new motivation, creativity and vision that you can adopt in both your professional and personal life.

You can also form amazing hobbies from volunteering e.g. you can volunteer to plant the community garden and love it so much that you plant your own garden.

Finding the right volunteer opportunity

There are many volunteer opportunities out there so the key is to find a position you would both enjoy and be capable of handling. Ask yourself important questions such as:

- Do I prefer to work with children, adults or animals?

- How much time am I capable of committing?

- Do I want to work as part of a team or alone?

- Which skills can I bring to the table?

- Which cause means the most to me?

The answer is your perfect volunteering job.

Some of the places you can find opportunities are libraries, service organizations, churches, museums, historical restorations, community theatres, sports teams etc.

Just visit different organizations and if you feel like you click with the staff and other volunteers, then go ahead and volunteer. You do not have to do it if you feel like something is off and you just don't feel it. Keep searching!

Chapter 10: Learning To Slow Down

"Nature does not hurry, yet everything is accomplished."~ Lao Tzu

Most of the time we tend to think that everything around us is too slow making us agitated and impatient and/or stressed while the truth is, we are just too fast. Building relationships, building a career, handling projects and tasks even eating can all be taken way too fast than they should giving us pressure which is certainly not healthy.

Let us look at some tips to help you slow down

Learn to live in the moment

Whatever you are doing now, give it your ultimate attention. If you are on a date with someone, engage them to make sure you are mentally there. If you are doing a project have mental checks on what you are actually doing and if you are having fun, let loose and enjoy every single moment- don't think about the pile of paperwork you have to work on by Wednesday.

Take a moment to Breathe

When you feel like you have a lot going on and you don't know what to do, simply stop, breath, relax and focus. We all feel this at one point in our lives. How did you cope?

There are a number of breathing techniques you could use. One popular one for elimination of stress and relaxation is the 4-7-8 where you breathe in for 4 seconds through the nose, hold that breath for 7 seconds and exhale for 8 seconds. You simply do this until you feel relaxed- and you will.

Drive slowly

It does not matter how fast you need to be there, just slow down. First, it will keep you safe and secondly you will enjoy the drive. We tend to be careless when we are distracted so as you drive focus on how you are driving and the scenery around you.

Learn to take small breaks

Develop the habit of taking some short breaks as you work. This recharges you and enables you to focus on the task, which increases your chances of doing it well.

Travel and explore

I know, I know, not everyone has the luxury of travelling. However, it doesn't take a lot to go somewhere you've never been even if it's in your own city for just a night e.g. a staycation or camping.

Travelling helps you slow down, recharge and have some fun- it helps us appreciate simple pleasures.

Conclusion

We have come to the end of the book. Thank you for reading and congratulations for reading until the end.

As you have read, changing your life and adopting good healthy habits is not so hard; however, it's important to be consistent to enjoy the amazing benefits these habits have to offer.

If you found the book valuable, can you recommend it to others? One way to do that is to post a review on Amazon.

Thank you and good luck!

Richard